The Masked Cleaning Ladies Mee...

JOHN COLDWELL

Illustrated by Joseph Sharples

OXFORD
UNIVERSITY PRESS

OXFORD
UNIVERSITY PRESS

Great Clarendon Street, Oxford OX2 6DP

Oxford University Press is a department of the University of Oxford.
It furthers the University's objective of excellence in research, scholarship,
and education by publishing worldwide in

Oxford   New York

Auckland   Cape Town   Dar es Salaam   Hong Kong   Karachi
Kuala Lumpur   Madrid   Melbourne   Mexico City   Nairobi
New Delhi   Shanghai   Taipei   Toronto

With offices in

Argentina   Austria   Brazil   Chile   Czech Republic   France   Greece
Guatemala   Hungary   Italy   Japan   Poland   Portugal   Singapore
South Korea   Switzerland   Thailand   Turkey   Ukraine   Vietnam

Oxford is a registered trade mark of Oxford University Press
in the UK and in certain other countries

Text © John Coldwell 1998

British Library Cataloguing in Publication Data
Data available

ISBN-13: 978-0-19-917967-1
ISBN-10: 0-19-917967-0

3 5 7 9 10 8 6 4 2

Available in packs
Stage 10 More Stories A Pack of 6:
ISBN-13: 978-0-19-917963-3; ISBN-10: 0-19-917963-8
Stage 10 More Stories A Class Pack:
ISBN-13: 978-0-19-917970-1; ISBN-10: 0-19-917970-0
Guided Reading Cards also available:
ISBN-13: 978-0-19-917972-5; ISBN-10: 0-19-917972-7

Cover artwork by Joseph Sharples
Photograph of John Coldwell © Caroline Scott Photography, Staplehurst

Printed in China by Imago

Queen Norah was showing Princess
Jane the Royal Treasures.

'Jane!' snapped Queen Norah.
'You aren't listening!'

'I am,' yawned Princess Jane.

'Then,' said Queen
Norah, 'what is this?'

She pointed at a model of a horse.

'It's er...' began the Princess.

'You're as bad as King Harry. He doesn't care about the Royal Treasures either. This is the Golden Horse of Tong. It belonged to your Great, Great, Great Grandfather. H...'

King Harry came in.

'The postman's just been,' he said. 'This is for you.'

Queen Norah opened the letter.

'Bad news,' sighed Queen Norah. 'My sister's crown is missing.'

'Stolen?' asked King Harry.

'I expect she's just put it down somewhere. You know what she's like. I shall have to go and help her find it.'

'What day is it?' said
Queen Norah.

'Monday?' said King Harry.

'Correct. The cleaning ladies
will be coming. The front of the
castle needs a jolly good scrub.
I want you to stay here and make
sure those cleaners do a good job.'

'Yes, dear,' said King Harry.

'I shall lock up the Royal
Treasures. I don't want our Royal
Treasures being lost or stolen.'

6

King Harry waved goodbye to Queen Norah.

'Now,' said King Harry to Captain Smith and Captain Jones. 'It's time for us to change into the Masked Cleaning Ladies of Om.'

The King and his two captains took over the housework when the last cleaner left. They kept it a secret from Queen Norah by dressing up as cleaning ladies and wearing masks. The Queen would have been furious if she ever found out.

A few moments later the three men came back, dressed as cleaning ladies.

'The Queen won't be back for ages,' said Princess Jane. 'You don't need to wear the masks today.'

2

'Ahoy there!' came a cry from outside the castle. 'We are a gang of very dangerous pirates, hiding behind a rock.'

Princess Jane peeped over the castle wall.

'Where's your ship?' she asked.

'We're saving up for one. Now give us your treasure.'

'No!' shouted King Harry.

'Then we will make you walk the plank,' yelled the voice.

'Have you got a plank?' called the King.

'No. We'll throw you to the sharks, then,' shouted the voice.

'There aren't any sharks round here,' called Princess Jane.

'Look,' shouted the voice. 'Just hand over your treasure.'

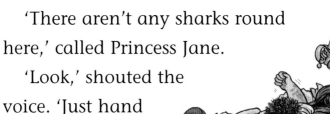

'We can't give them the Royal
Treasure,' said King Harry, 'because the
Queen has locked the room and she has
the key.'

'We will have to fight them,' said
Princess Jane.

'Fight?' said King Harry.

'You mean us?' gasped Captain Smith
and Captain Jones.

Princess Jane took out her telescope and looked at the rock.

'I can only see three pirates. They don't look fierce, but they are dirty.'

'Dirty!' said King Harry. 'The Masked Cleaning Ladies know about dirt. We shall need hot water, soap, polish and dusters.'

'You can't start cleaning now,' said Princess Jane.

'Ah,' said the King. 'This is a very special cleaning job. Captain Smith, go and polish the big shield in the main hall. Captain Jones, you must polish the floor. I shall run a nice, hot, soapy bath.'

'What shall I do?' asked Princess Jane.

'You keep them talking,' said the King.

A bit later King Harry yelled, 'OK, you dirty pirates, come and get us!'

The three pirates rushed out from behind the rock. They ran across the drawbridge. The doors opened.

The pirates stopped. There in front of them was a cleaning lady. She was armed only with a duster.

'This is going to be easy,' said the first pirate.

The pirates raced forward. The cleaning lady was really Captain Smith and he pulled his duster to one side. Beneath it was the royal shield. It was so shiny that the pirates were dazzled. They hid their eyes. They did not see the floor that Captain Jones had polished.

'Help!' yelled the pirates as they skidded on the slippery floor. They slid down the hall, straight into the bathroom.

The three pirates landed in a
lovely hot, soapy bath. Before they
had time to say, 'Ahoy there,' they
were being scrubbed and soaped.
  'Ow!'
  'Hold still!'

The pirates wiped the soap out of their eyes. They saw King Harry, Captain Smith and Captain Jones dressed as cleaning ladies and holding up mirrors.

'Oh no,' said the first pirate. 'We're clean.'

King Harry was holding a camera.

'Please don't take our picture,' said the pirates. 'It would be terrible if other pirates found out. Please, we'd do anything.'

'You have wasted a lot of our time,' said King Harry. 'Now, put these aprons on. You can help with the cleaning.'

'Cleaning?' said the pirates.

'Yes,' said King Harry. 'Or I'll take your picture.'

Soon, the King and his captains and the three pirates were all scrubbing away at the castle wall.

‘Tra da-da daaaa!’

A trumpet sounded.

‘Oh no,’ said King Harry. ‘That means that Queen Norah is back.’

‘She’ll find out that we are the cleaning ladies,’ said Captain Smith.

‘She’ll be furious,’ said Captain Jones.

‘What shall we do?’ wailed Captain Smith.

'There's only one thing we can do,' said King Harry. 'The three pirates must pretend to be the cleaners.'

'Good idea,' said Princess Jane. 'You go and get changed and I'll watch the pirates.'

The drawbridge was lowered. King Harry ran to meet Queen Norah.

'Did you find your sister's crown?' he asked.

'It was under the sofa,' said the Queen. She looked up and saw the three pirates scrubbing at the front wall of the castle.

'Those cleaners haven't got their masks on.'

'Er, uh, er,' gasped King Harry.

'I am glad. They have such honest faces,' said the Queen. 'Come down at once, you cleaners.'

The three pirates stood
before the Queen.

'What day is it?' said
the Queen.

'Monday?' said the pirates.

'Pay day,' laughed the Queen.

'Oh dear,' said King Harry.

'Oh yes,' said the pirates.

The Queen opened her purse. The
pirates held out their hands.

'But – ' began Captain Jones.

'Your majesty…' said Captain Smith.

'What a fuss,' said Queen Norah.
'Anyone would think that *you* had done
the cleaning. Now cleaners, come with
me. I was showing Jane the Royal
Treasures this morning. They need a
good polish.'

Queen Norah walked off with the
three pirates.

King Harry whispered to the two
captains, 'I don't trust those pirates.
Follow me.'

Queen Norah
unlocked the door.

'This is the room where we keep all the Royal Treasures,' she said proudly.

'Are they worth a lot of money?' asked the first pirate.

'This is the Golden Horse of Tong. It is worth thousands,' she said.

'Thousands, eh?' said the second pirate.

'When I come back,' said Queen Norah, 'I want to see those treasures shining.'

'Right lads,' said the first pirate. 'Let's grab the stuff.'

The pirates stuffed the treasures into their aprons. They ran towards the main door.

King Harry, Princess Jane and the two captains came out from behind the curtain.

'Not so fast!' said King Harry.

The pirates stood still.

'Give those Royal Treasures back at once!'

Sadly, the pirates took the treasures out of their aprons.

'Now,' said King Harry to Jane. 'Take those treasures back before the Queen finds out that they are missing.'

'I will,' said Jane. She dashed off carrying the treasures.

'Let's face it,' said King Harry. 'You are no good as pirates.'

One of the pirates began to sniff.

'Why don't you do something honest?' said Captain Smith.

'You made a very good job of cleaning the castle,' said King Harry. 'You should become cleaners.'

'That reminds me,' said Captain Jones. 'You still have the cleaning money. Hand it over.'

The first pirate gave him back the money.

'The pirates can have half,' said King Harry, 'because they did half the work.'

'Thanks very much,' said the first pirate.

'Cor,' said the second pirate. 'This is like doing a real job.'

'I was going to keep this,' said the third pirate. 'But you've been so kind.'

He handed King Harry the Golden Horse of Tong.

The pirates left.

A few moments later Queen Norah and Jane came running down the hall.

'Help! We've been robbed!' yelled Queen Norah. 'It's those cleaning ladies. They have stolen the Golden Horse of Tong!'

'Do you mean this?' said King Harry, holding out the Golden Horse.

'Oh, thank goodness,' she gasped. 'What are you doing with it?'

'Er – um,' said King Harry. Then he had an idea. 'Oh, yes. I remember. I was going to tell Jane all about it. It was given to King Sam by the people of Tong.'

'Oh, Harry,' smiled Queen Norah, 'so you and Jane do care about the Royal Treasures.'

'Of course we do,' said King Harry. 'We'd be heartbroken if they were ever lost.'

'Or stolen,' said Jane.

About the author

I was born in London in 1950 and now live by the seaside, in Ramsgate. In the evening I like to write stories and poems. I do this very quietly. Then I go downstairs and play jazz records very loudly. My family think that I do two very daft things. One is going up the garden every night looking for frogs, newts and hedgehogs. The other is supporting Gillingham Football Club.